Dear Sister

from you to me®

from you to me®

concept by Neil Coxon

Dear Sister

from you to me®

This book is for your Sister's unique story.

It is for her to capture some of her life's key memories, experiences and feelings.

Ask her to complete it carefully and, if she wants to, add some photographs or images to personalise it more.

When it is finished and returned to you, this will be a record of her story . . . a story that you will treasure forever.

Dear

Here is a gift from me to you . . . for you to give to me.

When we are children we are always asking questions . . . well I now have a few for you.

Please could you answer them in the way that only you know how and then give the book back to me.

There might be a couple of questions that you prefer not to answer, so don't worry, just answer the others as well as you can . . . I won't mind.

People say that we all have at least one book in us, and this will be one of yours.

The story of you and me that I will treasure forever.

Thank you,

with love

Tell me about the time and place you were born . . .

What are your **earliest** memories?

Tell me about your **childhood** ...

What do you think **people thought** about you as a child?

What do you remember about the place/s you lived when you were young?

What were your favourite childhood toys or games?

Tell me about your **best** childhood friend/s...

What do you remember about your holidays as a child?

What did you *enjoy* about your *school* days?

What did you want to do when you grew up?

Tell me about the hobbies you had when you were young . . .

What family traditions do you continue to follow?

Being the **eldest, youngest** or a **middle** sibling can be **different**.

Describe what it is like for you . . .

If you could, what would you swap with me?

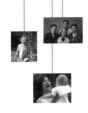

What family values have you learnt that you would like to pass on to others?

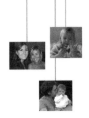

Tell me some of your favourite family stories . . .

Did you have an idol when you were young?
Tell me who and why . . .

Who was your first love and why?

What was the first piece of music you bought?

Tell me about your first job and some of the other work you have done . . .

Describe some of your fondest memories of the times we have spent together . . .

Describe the **funniest** things that have happened to us . . .

Tell me what you like about me . . .

What is the most **annoying** thing I have done?

Is there anything you would change about me?

What will you remember me for?

What would you still love us to do together?

What are the happiest or greatest memories of your life?

Tell me about the things that make you happy or laugh . . .

What piece/s of music would you choose in your own favourite 'top 10'?

Tell me what would make up your favourite meal ...

Describe your favourite way of spending a weekend ...

What would you include in your top 10 views in the world?

What have been some of your best holiday destinations?

If you could live anywhere ...
where would you live and why?

What are a few of your favourite things?

Describe your memory of some major world events that have happened in your lifetime . . .

If you could **travel** in **time** ...

where would you go to and why?

*the **from you to me** website is capturing some of the fascinating answers to this question . . . why not share your answer for others to read . . .*

send it to change@fromyoutome.com

Describe the greatest change that you have seen in your lifetime so far . . .

If you were an animal ... what type of animal would you be, and why?

If you won the Lottery . . . what would you do with the money?

Tell me about the goals and aspirations you have had for your life . . .

What do you still want to achieve in your life?

Is there anything you'd like to change about yourself?

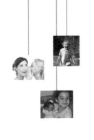

Tell me about the **dreams** you have for your life . . .

What can I do to help you achieve what you want?

What have you found most difficult in your life?

What is your **biggest regret** in your life?

Can you do anything about it **now**?

Is there anything you would like to say SORRY for?

With hindsight what would you do **differently**?

If you were granted **three wishes** . . .
what would they be and why?

Tell me something you think I won't know about you . . .

What would you like your epitaph to say?

What is the best piece of advice you have ever been given?

Given your experiences, what advice would you like to offer me?

And now your chance to write anything else you want to say to me . . .

These extra pages are for us to write any
questions, memories or **answers** that
may not have been covered elsewhere in the book . . .

And finally for the record . . .

what is your full name ?

what is your date of birth ?

what colour are your eyes ?

how tall are you ?

what blood group are you ?

what was the date when you completed this story for me ?

Dear *Sister*

I will treasure this book, your memories and your advice forever.

I hope you enjoyed answering my questions.

Thank you so much for doing it and for writing your own book about you and me . . .

from you to me

Dear *Sister*

from you to me®

First published in the UK by *from you to me*, April 2008
Copyright, *from you to me* limited 2008
Hackless House, Murhill, Bath, BA2 7FH
www.fromyoutome.com
E-mail: hello@fromyoutome.com

Cover design by so design consultants, Wick, Bristol   www.so-design.co.uk
Printed and bound in the UK by Cromwell Press, Trowbridge, Wiltshire

Mixed Sources
Product group from well-managed
forests and other controlled sources
www.fsc.org Cert no. TT-COC-2082
© 1996 Forest Stewardship Council
FSC

This paper is manufactured from material sourced
from forests certified according to strict
environmental, social and economical standards.

If you think other questions should be included in future editions, please let
us know. And remember to submit your answer to the question about 'the
greatest change' that has been seen to the *from you to me* website to let other
people read about these fascinating insights . . .

If you liked the concept of this book, please tell your family and friends and
look out for others in the *from you to me* range:

> **Dear Mum, *from you to me***
> **Dear Dad, *from you to me***
> **Dear Grandma, *from you to me***
> **Dear Grandad, *from you to me***
> **Dear Brother, *from you to me***
> **Dear Friend, *from you to me***
> other relationships and memory journals coming soon . . .